AF871137

MY

TRAVEL JOURNAL

KORIE HEROLD

Paige Tate & Co.

Paige Tate & Co.

My Travel Journal
Copyright © 2024 Korie Herold

Published in 2024 by Paige Tate & Co.
Paige Tate & Co. is an imprint of Blue Star Press
PO Box 8835, Bend, OR 97708
contact@paigetate.com | www.paigetate.com

The authorized representative in the EU for product safety and compliance is Authorised Rep Compliance Ltd., Ground Floor, 71 Lower Baggot Street, Dublin, D02 P593, Ireland. www.arccompliance.com

All rights reserved. No part of this publication may be reproduced or transmitted in any form or by any means, electronic or mechanical, including photocopy, recording or any information storage and retrieval system, without permission in writing from the publisher.

Map (pgs 2–3, 8–9) © pingebat / Adobe Stock
Illustrations and Design by Korie Herold

ISBN: 9781963183023
Printed in China

10 9 8 7 6 5 4

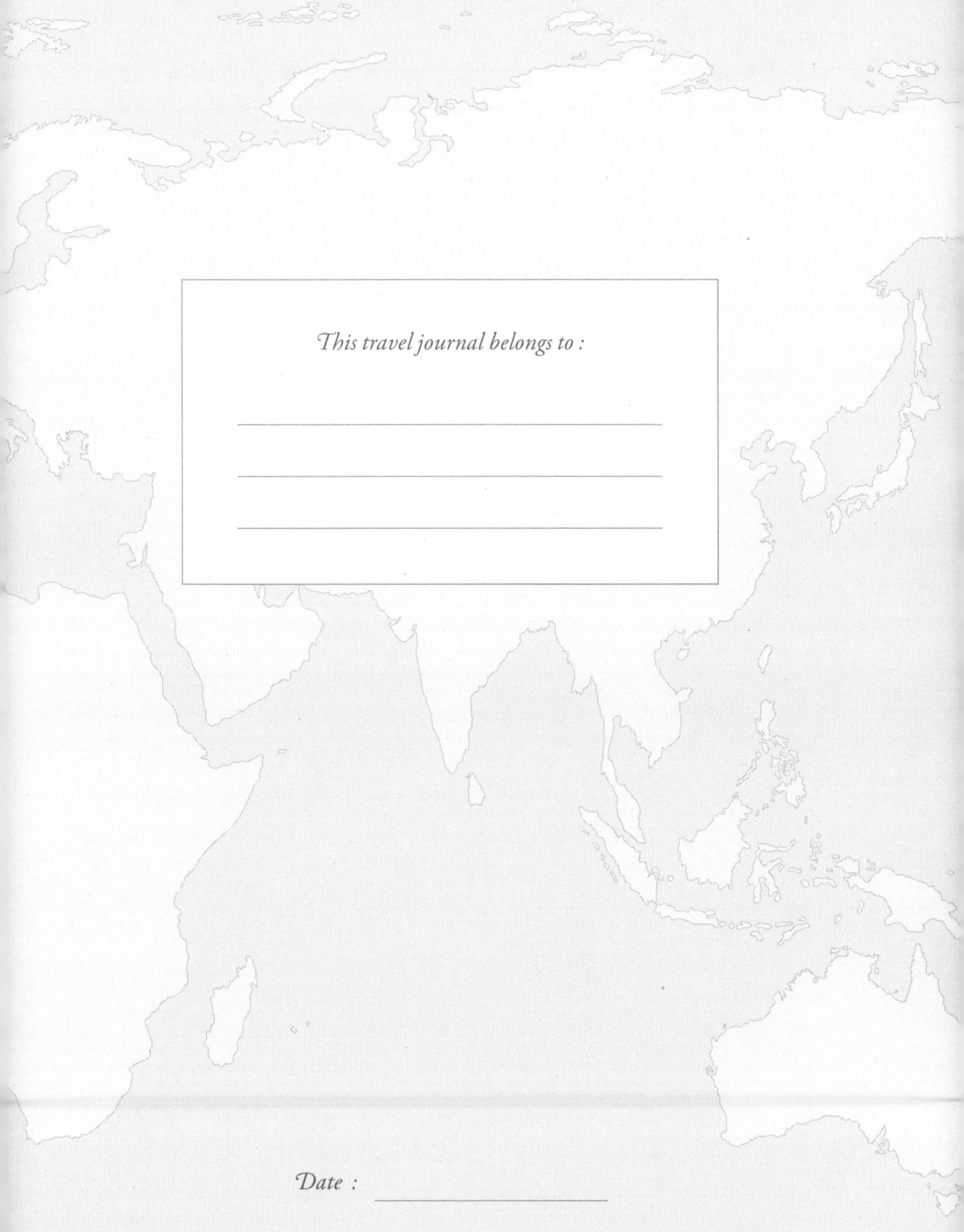

This travel journal belongs to :

Date :

TRAVEL INDEX

TRAVEL INDEX

INTRODUCTION

If you're holding this journal, chances are you've got a serious case of wanderlust and a passion for adventure!

This travel keepsake is designed to be your ultimate companion in preserving your most cherished travel memories in one place. Whether it's a meticulously planned international voyage years in the making or a spontaneous weekend road trip, every adventure deserves to be celebrated and remembered.

Think of this journal as your personal time capsule, allowing you to look back on your travel experiences in a meaningful and tangible way. I'd encourage you to use any pen, pencil, or marker you prefer. Fill the pages with photos, stickers, ticket stubs, and any other flat travel mementos that bring your journeys to life. Before you know it, this book will become a treasured heirloom, transporting you back to your adventures with every flip of the page.

With ample space to document 50 unique travel memories, each entry features thoughtfully designed prompts to fill out either during or after the trip. For best memory-keeping, I'd recommend filling out the prompts while the adventure is fresh on your mind, ensuring that no nuanced detail fades away.

The travel index at the beginning allows you to easily navigate your documented trips, while the additional pages at the back provide a creative space to showcase more photos, keepsakes, and free-form journaling. There's no right or wrong way to fill these pages—let your experiences and creativity guide you.

Tip: Photo stickers work great in this journal. You can have your photos printed onto stickers through various online printers, or you can purchase a portable photo sticker printer to use.

As you embark on your next adventure, make sure to pack this journal alongside your essentials. Embrace the journey, savor the moments, and let this book be your trusted companion along the way.

Onward and Upward,
Korie Herold

I would love to see *My Travel Journal* in your hands, documenting all your incredible adventures in traveling. Use #mytraveljournalBOOK and tag @korieherold to connect on social media.

PLACES I WANT TO GO SOMEDAY

PLACES I'VE BEEN

Mark all travel destinations on this map using your favorite colored pen or pencil. Add dates, people you traveled with, or your overall rating of the trip next to each place.

DESTINATION :

DATE(S) :

STAYED HERE :

☐ TRAVELED SOLO

☐ TRAVELED WITH OTHERS

TRIP HIGHLIGHTS :

•

•

•

MEMORABLE MEAL : ☐ IT WAS AMAZING ☐ IT WAS AWFUL

A MOMENT I'LL NEVER FORGET :

NEW EXPERIENCES OR LESSONS LEARNED :

MUSIC, SONGS, OR SOUNDS THAT REMIND ME OF THIS TRIP :

IF I COULD DO THIS TRIP OVER, HERE'S WHAT I'D DO DIFFERENTLY :

WHAT I'M GRATEFUL FOR ABOUT THIS JOURNEY :

HOW I'D RATE THIS TRIP : ☆☆☆☆☆	PLAN TO RETURN? ☐ YES ☐ NO

DESTINATION :

DATE(S) :

STAYED HERE :

☐ TRAVELED SOLO

☐ TRAVELED WITH OTHERS

TRIP HIGHLIGHTS :

-
-
-

MEMORABLE MEAL : ☐ IT WAS AMAZING ☐ IT WAS AWFUL

A MOMENT I'LL NEVER FORGET :

NEW EXPERIENCES OR LESSONS LEARNED :

MUSIC, SONGS, OR SOUNDS THAT REMIND ME OF THIS TRIP :

IF I COULD DO THIS TRIP OVER, HERE'S WHAT I'D DO DIFFERENTLY :

WHAT I'M GRATEFUL FOR ABOUT THIS JOURNEY :

HOW I'D RATE THIS TRIP : ☆☆☆☆☆	PLAN TO RETURN? ☐ YES ☐ NO

DESTINATION :	
DATE(S) :	
STAYED HERE :	☐ TRAVELED SOLO ☐ TRAVELED WITH OTHERS
TRIP HIGHLIGHTS : • • •	

MEMORABLE MEAL : ☐ IT WAS AMAZING ☐ IT WAS AWFUL

A MOMENT I'LL NEVER FORGET :

NEW EXPERIENCES OR LESSONS LEARNED :

MUSIC, SONGS, OR SOUNDS THAT REMIND ME OF THIS TRIP :

IF I COULD DO THIS TRIP OVER, HERE'S WHAT I'D DO DIFFERENTLY :

WHAT I'M GRATEFUL FOR ABOUT THIS JOURNEY :

HOW I'D RATE THIS TRIP : ☆☆☆☆☆	PLAN TO RETURN? ☐ YES ☐ NO

DESTINATION :
DATE(S) :

STAYED HERE :	☐ TRAVELED SOLO ☐ TRAVELED WITH OTHERS

TRIP HIGHLIGHTS :

-
-
-

MEMORABLE MEAL : ☐ IT WAS AMAZING ☐ IT WAS AWFUL

A MOMENT I'LL NEVER FORGET :

NEW EXPERIENCES OR LESSONS LEARNED :

MUSIC, SONGS, OR SOUNDS THAT REMIND ME OF THIS TRIP :

IF I COULD DO THIS TRIP OVER, HERE'S WHAT I'D DO DIFFERENTLY :

WHAT I'M GRATEFUL FOR ABOUT THIS JOURNEY :

HOW I'D RATE THIS TRIP : ☆☆☆☆☆	PLAN TO RETURN? ☐ YES ☐ NO

DESTINATION :

DATE(S) :

STAYED HERE :

☐ TRAVELED SOLO

☐ TRAVELED WITH OTHERS

TRIP HIGHLIGHTS :

-
-
-

MEMORABLE MEAL : ☐ IT WAS AMAZING ☐ IT WAS AWFUL

A MOMENT I'LL NEVER FORGET :

NEW EXPERIENCES OR LESSONS LEARNED :

MUSIC, SONGS, OR SOUNDS THAT REMIND ME OF THIS TRIP :

IF I COULD DO THIS TRIP OVER, HERE'S WHAT I'D DO DIFFERENTLY :

WHAT I'M GRATEFUL FOR ABOUT THIS JOURNEY :

HOW I'D RATE THIS TRIP : ☆☆☆☆☆	PLAN TO RETURN? ☐ YES ☐ NO

DESTINATION :

DATE(S) :

STAYED HERE :

☐ TRAVELED SOLO

☐ TRAVELED WITH OTHERS

TRIP HIGHLIGHTS :

-
-
-

MEMORABLE MEAL : ☐ IT WAS AMAZING ☐ IT WAS AWFUL

A MOMENT I'LL NEVER FORGET :

NEW EXPERIENCES OR LESSONS LEARNED :

MUSIC, SONGS, OR SOUNDS THAT REMIND ME OF THIS TRIP :

IF I COULD DO THIS TRIP OVER, HERE'S WHAT I'D DO DIFFERENTLY :

WHAT I'M GRATEFUL FOR ABOUT THIS JOURNEY :

HOW I'D RATE THIS TRIP : ☆☆☆☆☆	PLAN TO RETURN? ☐ YES ☐ NO

DESTINATION :	
DATE(S) :	
STAYED HERE :	☐ TRAVELED SOLO ☐ TRAVELED WITH OTHERS
TRIP HIGHLIGHTS : • • •	

MEMORABLE MEAL : ☐ IT WAS AMAZING ☐ IT WAS AWFUL

A MOMENT I'LL NEVER FORGET :

NEW EXPERIENCES OR LESSONS LEARNED :

MUSIC, SONGS, OR SOUNDS THAT REMIND ME OF THIS TRIP :

IF I COULD DO THIS TRIP OVER, HERE'S WHAT I'D DO DIFFERENTLY :

WHAT I'M GRATEFUL FOR ABOUT THIS JOURNEY :

HOW I'D RATE THIS TRIP : ☆ ☆ ☆ ☆ ☆	PLAN TO RETURN? ☐ YES ☐ NO

DESTINATION :

DATE(S) :

STAYED HERE :

☐ TRAVELED SOLO

☐ TRAVELED WITH OTHERS

TRIP HIGHLIGHTS :

-
-
-

MEMORABLE MEAL : ☐ IT WAS AMAZING ☐ IT WAS AWFUL

A MOMENT I'LL NEVER FORGET :

NEW EXPERIENCES OR LESSONS LEARNED :

MUSIC, SONGS, OR SOUNDS THAT REMIND ME OF THIS TRIP :

IF I COULD DO THIS TRIP OVER, HERE'S WHAT I'D DO DIFFERENTLY :

WHAT I'M GRATEFUL FOR ABOUT THIS JOURNEY :

HOW I'D RATE THIS TRIP : ☆ ☆ ☆ ☆ ☆	PLAN TO RETURN? ☐ YES ☐ NO

DESTINATION :

DATE(S) :

STAYED HERE :

☐ TRAVELED SOLO

☐ TRAVELED WITH OTHERS

TRIP HIGHLIGHTS :

-
-
-

MEMORABLE MEAL : ☐ IT WAS AMAZING ☐ IT WAS AWFUL

A MOMENT I'LL NEVER FORGET :

NEW EXPERIENCES OR LESSONS LEARNED :

MUSIC, SONGS, OR SOUNDS THAT REMIND ME OF THIS TRIP :

IF I COULD DO THIS TRIP OVER, HERE'S WHAT I'D DO DIFFERENTLY :

WHAT I'M GRATEFUL FOR ABOUT THIS JOURNEY :

HOW I'D RATE THIS TRIP : ☆☆☆☆☆	PLAN TO RETURN? ☐ YES ☐ NO

DESTINATION :	
DATE(S) :	
STAYED HERE :	☐ TRAVELED SOLO ☐ TRAVELED WITH OTHERS
TRIP HIGHLIGHTS : • • •	

MEMORABLE MEAL : ☐ IT WAS AMAZING ☐ IT WAS AWFUL

A MOMENT I'LL NEVER FORGET :

NEW EXPERIENCES OR LESSONS LEARNED :

MUSIC, SONGS, OR SOUNDS THAT REMIND ME OF THIS TRIP :

IF I COULD DO THIS TRIP OVER, HERE'S WHAT I'D DO DIFFERENTLY :

WHAT I'M GRATEFUL FOR ABOUT THIS JOURNEY :

HOW I'D RATE THIS TRIP : ☆☆☆☆☆	PLAN TO RETURN? ☐ YES ☐ NO

DESTINATION :	
DATE(S) :	
STAYED HERE :	☐ TRAVELED SOLO ☐ TRAVELED WITH OTHERS
TRIP HIGHLIGHTS : • • •	

MEMORABLE MEAL : ☐ IT WAS AMAZING ☐ IT WAS AWFUL

A MOMENT I'LL NEVER FORGET :

NEW EXPERIENCES OR LESSONS LEARNED :

MUSIC, SONGS, OR SOUNDS THAT REMIND ME OF THIS TRIP :

IF I COULD DO THIS TRIP OVER, HERE'S WHAT I'D DO DIFFERENTLY :

WHAT I'M GRATEFUL FOR ABOUT THIS JOURNEY :

HOW I'D RATE THIS TRIP : ☆ ☆ ☆ ☆ ☆	PLAN TO RETURN? ☐ YES ☐ NO

DESTINATION :

DATE(S) :

STAYED HERE :

☐ TRAVELED SOLO

☐ TRAVELED WITH OTHERS

TRIP HIGHLIGHTS :

-
-
-

MEMORABLE MEAL : ☐ IT WAS AMAZING ☐ IT WAS AWFUL

A MOMENT I'LL NEVER FORGET :

NEW EXPERIENCES OR LESSONS LEARNED :

MUSIC, SONGS, OR SOUNDS THAT REMIND ME OF THIS TRIP :

IF I COULD DO THIS TRIP OVER, HERE'S WHAT I'D DO DIFFERENTLY :

WHAT I'M GRATEFUL FOR ABOUT THIS JOURNEY :

HOW I'D RATE THIS TRIP : ☆☆☆☆☆	PLAN TO RETURN? ☐ YES ☐ NO

DESTINATION :	
DATE(S) :	
STAYED HERE :	☐ TRAVELED SOLO ☐ TRAVELED WITH OTHERS
TRIP HIGHLIGHTS : • • •	

MEMORABLE MEAL : ☐ IT WAS AMAZING ☐ IT WAS AWFUL

A MOMENT I'LL NEVER FORGET :

NEW EXPERIENCES OR LESSONS LEARNED :

MUSIC, SONGS, OR SOUNDS THAT REMIND ME OF THIS TRIP :

IF I COULD DO THIS TRIP OVER, HERE'S WHAT I'D DO DIFFERENTLY :

WHAT I'M GRATEFUL FOR ABOUT THIS JOURNEY :

HOW I'D RATE THIS TRIP : ☆ ☆ ☆ ☆ ☆	PLAN TO RETURN? ☐ YES ☐ NO

DESTINATION :

DATE(S) :

STAYED HERE :

☐ TRAVELED SOLO

☐ TRAVELED WITH OTHERS

TRIP HIGHLIGHTS :

-
-
-

MEMORABLE MEAL : ☐ IT WAS AMAZING ☐ IT WAS AWFUL

A MOMENT I'LL NEVER FORGET :

NEW EXPERIENCES OR LESSONS LEARNED :

MUSIC, SONGS, OR SOUNDS THAT REMIND ME OF THIS TRIP :

IF I COULD DO THIS TRIP OVER, HERE'S WHAT I'D DO DIFFERENTLY :

WHAT I'M GRATEFUL FOR ABOUT THIS JOURNEY :

HOW I'D RATE THIS TRIP : ☆ ☆ ☆ ☆ ☆	PLAN TO RETURN? ☐ YES ☐ NO

DESTINATION :

DATE(S) :

STAYED HERE :

☐ TRAVELED SOLO

☐ TRAVELED WITH OTHERS

TRIP HIGHLIGHTS :

-
-
-

MEMORABLE MEAL : ☐ IT WAS AMAZING ☐ IT WAS AWFUL

A MOMENT I'LL NEVER FORGET :

NEW EXPERIENCES OR LESSONS LEARNED :

MUSIC, SONGS, OR SOUNDS THAT REMIND ME OF THIS TRIP :

IF I COULD DO THIS TRIP OVER, HERE'S WHAT I'D DO DIFFERENTLY :

WHAT I'M GRATEFUL FOR ABOUT THIS JOURNEY :

HOW I'D RATE THIS TRIP : ☆☆☆☆☆	PLAN TO RETURN? ☐ YES ☐ NO

DESTINATION :

DATE(S) :

STAYED HERE :

☐ TRAVELED SOLO

☐ TRAVELED WITH OTHERS

TRIP HIGHLIGHTS :

•

•

•

MEMORABLE MEAL : ☐ IT WAS AMAZING ☐ IT WAS AWFUL

A MOMENT I'LL NEVER FORGET :

NEW EXPERIENCES OR LESSONS LEARNED :

MUSIC, SONGS, OR SOUNDS THAT REMIND ME OF THIS TRIP :

IF I COULD DO THIS TRIP OVER, HERE'S WHAT I'D DO DIFFERENTLY :

WHAT I'M GRATEFUL FOR ABOUT THIS JOURNEY :

HOW I'D RATE THIS TRIP : ☆☆☆☆☆	PLAN TO RETURN? ☐ YES ☐ NO

DESTINATION :	
DATE(S) :	
STAYED HERE :	☐ TRAVELED SOLO ☐ TRAVELED WITH OTHERS
TRIP HIGHLIGHTS : • • •	

MEMORABLE MEAL : ☐ IT WAS AMAZING ☐ IT WAS AWFUL

A MOMENT I'LL NEVER FORGET :

NEW EXPERIENCES OR LESSONS LEARNED :

MUSIC, SONGS, OR SOUNDS THAT REMIND ME OF THIS TRIP :

IF I COULD DO THIS TRIP OVER, HERE'S WHAT I'D DO DIFFERENTLY :

WHAT I'M GRATEFUL FOR ABOUT THIS JOURNEY :

HOW I'D RATE THIS TRIP : ☆☆☆☆☆	PLAN TO RETURN? ☐ YES ☐ NO

DESTINATION :

DATE(S) :

STAYED HERE :

☐ TRAVELED SOLO

☐ TRAVELED WITH OTHERS

TRIP HIGHLIGHTS :

-
-
-

MEMORABLE MEAL : ☐ IT WAS AMAZING ☐ IT WAS AWFUL

A MOMENT I'LL NEVER FORGET :

NEW EXPERIENCES OR LESSONS LEARNED :

MUSIC, SONGS, OR SOUNDS THAT REMIND ME OF THIS TRIP :

IF I COULD DO THIS TRIP OVER, HERE'S WHAT I'D DO DIFFERENTLY :

WHAT I'M GRATEFUL FOR ABOUT THIS JOURNEY :

HOW I'D RATE THIS TRIP : ☆☆☆☆☆	PLAN TO RETURN? ☐ YES ☐ NO

DESTINATION :
DATE(S) :

STAYED HERE :	☐ TRAVELED SOLO ☐ TRAVELED WITH OTHERS

TRIP HIGHLIGHTS :

-
-
-

MEMORABLE MEAL : ☐ IT WAS AMAZING ☐ IT WAS AWFUL

A MOMENT I'LL NEVER FORGET :

NEW EXPERIENCES OR LESSONS LEARNED :

MUSIC, SONGS, OR SOUNDS THAT REMIND ME OF THIS TRIP :

IF I COULD DO THIS TRIP OVER, HERE'S WHAT I'D DO DIFFERENTLY :

WHAT I'M GRATEFUL FOR ABOUT THIS JOURNEY :

HOW I'D RATE THIS TRIP : ☆ ☆ ☆ ☆ ☆	PLAN TO RETURN? ☐ YES ☐ NO

DESTINATION :

DATE(S) :

STAYED HERE :

☐ TRAVELED SOLO

☐ TRAVELED WITH OTHERS

TRIP HIGHLIGHTS :

-
-
-

MEMORABLE MEAL : ☐ IT WAS AMAZING ☐ IT WAS AWFUL

A MOMENT I'LL NEVER FORGET :

NEW EXPERIENCES OR LESSONS LEARNED :

MUSIC, SONGS, OR SOUNDS THAT REMIND ME OF THIS TRIP :

IF I COULD DO THIS TRIP OVER, HERE'S WHAT I'D DO DIFFERENTLY :

WHAT I'M GRATEFUL FOR ABOUT THIS JOURNEY :

HOW I'D RATE THIS TRIP : ☆☆☆☆☆	PLAN TO RETURN? ☐ YES ☐ NO

DESTINATION :

DATE(S) :

STAYED HERE :

☐ TRAVELED SOLO

☐ TRAVELED WITH OTHERS

TRIP HIGHLIGHTS :

-
-
-

MEMORABLE MEAL : ☐ IT WAS AMAZING ☐ IT WAS AWFUL

A MOMENT I'LL NEVER FORGET :

NEW EXPERIENCES OR LESSONS LEARNED :

MUSIC, SONGS, OR SOUNDS THAT REMIND ME OF THIS TRIP :

IF I COULD DO THIS TRIP OVER, HERE'S WHAT I'D DO DIFFERENTLY :

WHAT I'M GRATEFUL FOR ABOUT THIS JOURNEY :

HOW I'D RATE THIS TRIP : ☆ ☆ ☆ ☆ ☆	PLAN TO RETURN? ☐ YES ☐ NO

DESTINATION :

DATE(S) :

STAYED HERE :

☐ TRAVELED SOLO

☐ TRAVELED WITH OTHERS

TRIP HIGHLIGHTS :

-
-
-

MEMORABLE MEAL : ☐ IT WAS AMAZING ☐ IT WAS AWFUL

A MOMENT I'LL NEVER FORGET :

NEW EXPERIENCES OR LESSONS LEARNED :

MUSIC, SONGS, OR SOUNDS THAT REMIND ME OF THIS TRIP :

IF I COULD DO THIS TRIP OVER, HERE'S WHAT I'D DO DIFFERENTLY :

WHAT I'M GRATEFUL FOR ABOUT THIS JOURNEY :

HOW I'D RATE THIS TRIP : ☆☆☆☆☆	PLAN TO RETURN? ☐ YES ☐ NO

DESTINATION :

DATE(S) :

STAYED HERE :

☐ TRAVELED SOLO

☐ TRAVELED WITH OTHERS

TRIP HIGHLIGHTS :

-
-
-

MEMORABLE MEAL : ☐ IT WAS AMAZING ☐ IT WAS AWFUL

A MOMENT I'LL NEVER FORGET :

NEW EXPERIENCES OR LESSONS LEARNED :

MUSIC, SONGS, OR SOUNDS THAT REMIND ME OF THIS TRIP :

IF I COULD DO THIS TRIP OVER, HERE'S WHAT I'D DO DIFFERENTLY :

WHAT I'M GRATEFUL FOR ABOUT THIS JOURNEY :

HOW I'D RATE THIS TRIP : ☆☆☆☆☆	PLAN TO RETURN? ☐ YES ☐ NO

DESTINATION :

DATE(S) :

STAYED HERE :

☐ TRAVELED SOLO

☐ TRAVELED WITH OTHERS

TRIP HIGHLIGHTS :

-
-
-

MEMORABLE MEAL : ☐ IT WAS AMAZING ☐ IT WAS AWFUL

A MOMENT I'LL NEVER FORGET :

NEW EXPERIENCES OR LESSONS LEARNED :

MUSIC, SONGS, OR SOUNDS THAT REMIND ME OF THIS TRIP :

IF I COULD DO THIS TRIP OVER, HERE'S WHAT I'D DO DIFFERENTLY :

WHAT I'M GRATEFUL FOR ABOUT THIS JOURNEY :

HOW I'D RATE THIS TRIP : ☆ ☆ ☆ ☆ ☆	PLAN TO RETURN? ☐ YES ☐ NO

DESTINATION :

DATE(S) :

STAYED HERE :

☐ TRAVELED SOLO

☐ TRAVELED WITH OTHERS

TRIP HIGHLIGHTS :

•

•

•

MEMORABLE MEAL : ☐ IT WAS AMAZING ☐ IT WAS AWFUL

A MOMENT I'LL NEVER FORGET :

NEW EXPERIENCES OR LESSONS LEARNED :

MUSIC, SONGS, OR SOUNDS THAT REMIND ME OF THIS TRIP :

IF I COULD DO THIS TRIP OVER, HERE'S WHAT I'D DO DIFFERENTLY :

WHAT I'M GRATEFUL FOR ABOUT THIS JOURNEY :

HOW I'D RATE THIS TRIP : ☆☆☆☆☆	PLAN TO RETURN? ☐ YES ☐ NO

DESTINATION :	
DATE(S) :	
STAYED HERE :	☐ TRAVELED SOLO ☐ TRAVELED WITH OTHERS
TRIP HIGHLIGHTS : • • •	

MEMORABLE MEAL : ☐ IT WAS AMAZING ☐ IT WAS AWFUL

A MOMENT I'LL NEVER FORGET :

NEW EXPERIENCES OR LESSONS LEARNED :

MUSIC, SONGS, OR SOUNDS THAT REMIND ME OF THIS TRIP :

IF I COULD DO THIS TRIP OVER, HERE'S WHAT I'D DO DIFFERENTLY :

WHAT I'M GRATEFUL FOR ABOUT THIS JOURNEY :

HOW I'D RATE THIS TRIP : ☆☆☆☆☆	PLAN TO RETURN? ☐ YES ☐ NO

DESTINATION :
DATE(S) :

STAYED HERE :	☐ TRAVELED SOLO ☐ TRAVELED WITH OTHERS

TRIP HIGHLIGHTS :

-
-
-

MEMORABLE MEAL : ☐ IT WAS AMAZING ☐ IT WAS AWFUL

A MOMENT I'LL NEVER FORGET :

NEW EXPERIENCES OR LESSONS LEARNED :

MUSIC, SONGS, OR SOUNDS THAT REMIND ME OF THIS TRIP :

IF I COULD DO THIS TRIP OVER, HERE'S WHAT I'D DO DIFFERENTLY :

WHAT I'M GRATEFUL FOR ABOUT THIS JOURNEY :

HOW I'D RATE THIS TRIP : ☆☆☆☆☆	PLAN TO RETURN? ☐ YES ☐ NO

DESTINATION :

DATE(S) :

STAYED HERE :

☐ TRAVELED SOLO

☐ TRAVELED WITH OTHERS

TRIP HIGHLIGHTS :

-
-
-

MEMORABLE MEAL : ☐ IT WAS AMAZING ☐ IT WAS AWFUL

A MOMENT I'LL NEVER FORGET :

NEW EXPERIENCES OR LESSONS LEARNED :

MUSIC, SONGS, OR SOUNDS THAT REMIND ME OF THIS TRIP :

IF I COULD DO THIS TRIP OVER, HERE'S WHAT I'D DO DIFFERENTLY :

WHAT I'M GRATEFUL FOR ABOUT THIS JOURNEY :

HOW I'D RATE THIS TRIP : ☆☆☆☆☆	PLAN TO RETURN? ☐ YES ☐ NO

DESTINATION :

DATE(S) :

STAYED HERE :

☐ TRAVELED SOLO

☐ TRAVELED WITH OTHERS

TRIP HIGHLIGHTS :

-
-
-

MEMORABLE MEAL : ☐ IT WAS AMAZING ☐ IT WAS AWFUL

A MOMENT I'LL NEVER FORGET :

NEW EXPERIENCES OR LESSONS LEARNED :

MUSIC, SONGS, OR SOUNDS THAT REMIND ME OF THIS TRIP :

IF I COULD DO THIS TRIP OVER, HERE'S WHAT I'D DO DIFFERENTLY :

WHAT I'M GRATEFUL FOR ABOUT THIS JOURNEY :

HOW I'D RATE THIS TRIP : ☆☆☆☆☆	PLAN TO RETURN? ☐ YES ☐ NO

DESTINATION :

DATE(S) :

STAYED HERE :

☐ TRAVELED SOLO

☐ TRAVELED WITH OTHERS

TRIP HIGHLIGHTS :

-
-
-

MEMORABLE MEAL : ☐ IT WAS AMAZING ☐ IT WAS AWFUL

A MOMENT I'LL NEVER FORGET :

NEW EXPERIENCES OR LESSONS LEARNED :

MUSIC, SONGS, OR SOUNDS THAT REMIND ME OF THIS TRIP :

IF I COULD DO THIS TRIP OVER, HERE'S WHAT I'D DO DIFFERENTLY :

WHAT I'M GRATEFUL FOR ABOUT THIS JOURNEY :

HOW I'D RATE THIS TRIP : ☆☆☆☆☆	PLAN TO RETURN? ☐ YES ☐ NO

DESTINATION :

DATE(S) :

STAYED HERE :

☐ TRAVELED SOLO

☐ TRAVELED WITH OTHERS

TRIP HIGHLIGHTS :

-
-
-

MEMORABLE MEAL : ☐ IT WAS AMAZING ☐ IT WAS AWFUL

A MOMENT I'LL NEVER FORGET :

NEW EXPERIENCES OR LESSONS LEARNED :

MUSIC, SONGS, OR SOUNDS THAT REMIND ME OF THIS TRIP :

IF I COULD DO THIS TRIP OVER, HERE'S WHAT I'D DO DIFFERENTLY :

WHAT I'M GRATEFUL FOR ABOUT THIS JOURNEY :

HOW I'D RATE THIS TRIP : ☆☆☆☆☆	PLAN TO RETURN? ☐ YES ☐ NO

DESTINATION :

DATE(S) :

STAYED HERE :

☐ TRAVELED SOLO

☐ TRAVELED WITH OTHERS

TRIP HIGHLIGHTS :

•

•

•

MEMORABLE MEAL : ☐ IT WAS AMAZING ☐ IT WAS AWFUL

A MOMENT I'LL NEVER FORGET :

NEW EXPERIENCES OR LESSONS LEARNED :

MUSIC, SONGS, OR SOUNDS THAT REMIND ME OF THIS TRIP :

IF I COULD DO THIS TRIP OVER, HERE'S WHAT I'D DO DIFFERENTLY :

WHAT I'M GRATEFUL FOR ABOUT THIS JOURNEY :

HOW I'D RATE THIS TRIP : ☆☆☆☆☆	PLAN TO RETURN? ☐ YES ☐ NO

DESTINATION :

DATE(S) :

STAYED HERE :

☐ TRAVELED SOLO

☐ TRAVELED WITH OTHERS

TRIP HIGHLIGHTS :

-
-
-

MEMORABLE MEAL : ☐ IT WAS AMAZING ☐ IT WAS AWFUL

A MOMENT I'LL NEVER FORGET :

NEW EXPERIENCES OR LESSONS LEARNED :

MUSIC, SONGS, OR SOUNDS THAT REMIND ME OF THIS TRIP :

IF I COULD DO THIS TRIP OVER, HERE'S WHAT I'D DO DIFFERENTLY :

WHAT I'M GRATEFUL FOR ABOUT THIS JOURNEY :

HOW I'D RATE THIS TRIP : ☆☆☆☆☆	PLAN TO RETURN? ☐ YES ☐ NO

DESTINATION :	
DATE(S) :	
STAYED HERE :	☐ TRAVELED SOLO ☐ TRAVELED WITH OTHERS
TRIP HIGHLIGHTS : • • •	

MEMORABLE MEAL : ☐ IT WAS AMAZING ☐ IT WAS AWFUL

A MOMENT I'LL NEVER FORGET :

NEW EXPERIENCES OR LESSONS LEARNED :

MUSIC, SONGS, OR SOUNDS THAT REMIND ME OF THIS TRIP :

IF I COULD DO THIS TRIP OVER, HERE'S WHAT I'D DO DIFFERENTLY :

WHAT I'M GRATEFUL FOR ABOUT THIS JOURNEY :

HOW I'D RATE THIS TRIP : ☆ ☆ ☆ ☆ ☆	PLAN TO RETURN? ☐ YES ☐ NO

DESTINATION :	
DATE(S) :	
STAYED HERE :	☐ TRAVELED SOLO ☐ TRAVELED WITH OTHERS
TRIP HIGHLIGHTS : • • •	

MEMORABLE MEAL : ☐ IT WAS AMAZING ☐ IT WAS AWFUL

A MOMENT I'LL NEVER FORGET :

NEW EXPERIENCES OR LESSONS LEARNED :

MUSIC, SONGS, OR SOUNDS THAT REMIND ME OF THIS TRIP :

IF I COULD DO THIS TRIP OVER, HERE'S WHAT I'D DO DIFFERENTLY :

WHAT I'M GRATEFUL FOR ABOUT THIS JOURNEY :

HOW I'D RATE THIS TRIP : ☆ ☆ ☆ ☆ ☆	PLAN TO RETURN? ☐ YES ☐ NO

DESTINATION :

DATE(S) :

STAYED HERE :

☐ TRAVELED SOLO

☐ TRAVELED WITH OTHERS

TRIP HIGHLIGHTS :

-
-
-

MEMORABLE MEAL : ☐ IT WAS AMAZING ☐ IT WAS AWFUL

A MOMENT I'LL NEVER FORGET :

NEW EXPERIENCES OR LESSONS LEARNED :

MUSIC, SONGS, OR SOUNDS THAT REMIND ME OF THIS TRIP :

IF I COULD DO THIS TRIP OVER, HERE'S WHAT I'D DO DIFFERENTLY :

WHAT I'M GRATEFUL FOR ABOUT THIS JOURNEY :

HOW I'D RATE THIS TRIP : ☆☆☆☆☆	PLAN TO RETURN? ☐ YES ☐ NO

DESTINATION :

DATE(S) :

STAYED HERE :

☐ TRAVELED SOLO

☐ TRAVELED WITH OTHERS

TRIP HIGHLIGHTS :

-
-
-

MEMORABLE MEAL : ☐ IT WAS AMAZING ☐ IT WAS AWFUL

A MOMENT I'LL NEVER FORGET :

NEW EXPERIENCES OR LESSONS LEARNED :

MUSIC, SONGS, OR SOUNDS THAT REMIND ME OF THIS TRIP :

IF I COULD DO THIS TRIP OVER, HERE'S WHAT I'D DO DIFFERENTLY :

WHAT I'M GRATEFUL FOR ABOUT THIS JOURNEY :

HOW I'D RATE THIS TRIP : ☆☆☆☆☆	PLAN TO RETURN? ☐ YES ☐ NO

DESTINATION :

DATE(S) :

STAYED HERE :

☐ TRAVELED SOLO

☐ TRAVELED WITH OTHERS

TRIP HIGHLIGHTS :

-
-
-

MEMORABLE MEAL : ☐ IT WAS AMAZING ☐ IT WAS AWFUL

A MOMENT I'LL NEVER FORGET :

NEW EXPERIENCES OR LESSONS LEARNED :

MUSIC, SONGS, OR SOUNDS THAT REMIND ME OF THIS TRIP :

IF I COULD DO THIS TRIP OVER, HERE'S WHAT I'D DO DIFFERENTLY :

WHAT I'M GRATEFUL FOR ABOUT THIS JOURNEY :

HOW I'D RATE THIS TRIP : ☆ ☆ ☆ ☆ ☆	PLAN TO RETURN? ☐ YES ☐ NO

DESTINATION :
DATE(S) :

STAYED HERE :	☐ TRAVELED SOLO ☐ TRAVELED WITH OTHERS

TRIP HIGHLIGHTS :

-
-
-

MEMORABLE MEAL : ☐ IT WAS AMAZING ☐ IT WAS AWFUL

A MOMENT I'LL NEVER FORGET :

NEW EXPERIENCES OR LESSONS LEARNED :

MUSIC, SONGS, OR SOUNDS THAT REMIND ME OF THIS TRIP :

IF I COULD DO THIS TRIP OVER, HERE'S WHAT I'D DO DIFFERENTLY :

WHAT I'M GRATEFUL FOR ABOUT THIS JOURNEY :

HOW I'D RATE THIS TRIP : ☆ ☆ ☆ ☆ ☆	PLAN TO RETURN? ☐ YES ☐ NO

DESTINATION :

DATE(S) :

STAYED HERE :

☐ TRAVELED SOLO

☐ TRAVELED WITH OTHERS

TRIP HIGHLIGHTS :

-
-
-

MEMORABLE MEAL : ☐ IT WAS AMAZING ☐ IT WAS AWFUL

A MOMENT I'LL NEVER FORGET :

NEW EXPERIENCES OR LESSONS LEARNED :

MUSIC, SONGS, OR SOUNDS THAT REMIND ME OF THIS TRIP :

IF I COULD DO THIS TRIP OVER, HERE'S WHAT I'D DO DIFFERENTLY :

WHAT I'M GRATEFUL FOR ABOUT THIS JOURNEY :

HOW I'D RATE THIS TRIP : ☆ ☆ ☆ ☆ ☆	PLAN TO RETURN? ☐ YES ☐ NO

DESTINATION :

DATE(S) :

STAYED HERE :

☐ TRAVELED SOLO

☐ TRAVELED WITH OTHERS

TRIP HIGHLIGHTS :

-
-
-

MEMORABLE MEAL : ☐ IT WAS AMAZING ☐ IT WAS AWFUL

A MOMENT I'LL NEVER FORGET :

NEW EXPERIENCES OR LESSONS LEARNED :

MUSIC, SONGS, OR SOUNDS THAT REMIND ME OF THIS TRIP :

IF I COULD DO THIS TRIP OVER, HERE'S WHAT I'D DO DIFFERENTLY :

WHAT I'M GRATEFUL FOR ABOUT THIS JOURNEY :

HOW I'D RATE THIS TRIP : ☆☆☆☆☆	PLAN TO RETURN? ☐ YES ☐ NO

DESTINATION :

DATE(S) :

STAYED HERE :

☐ TRAVELED SOLO

☐ TRAVELED WITH OTHERS

TRIP HIGHLIGHTS :

-
-
-

MEMORABLE MEAL : ☐ IT WAS AMAZING ☐ IT WAS AWFUL

A MOMENT I'LL NEVER FORGET :

NEW EXPERIENCES OR LESSONS LEARNED :

MUSIC, SONGS, OR SOUNDS THAT REMIND ME OF THIS TRIP :

IF I COULD DO THIS TRIP OVER, HERE'S WHAT I'D DO DIFFERENTLY :

WHAT I'M GRATEFUL FOR ABOUT THIS JOURNEY :

HOW I'D RATE THIS TRIP : ☆ ☆ ☆ ☆ ☆	PLAN TO RETURN? ☐ YES ☐ NO

DESTINATION :
DATE(S) :

STAYED HERE :	☐ TRAVELED SOLO ☐ TRAVELED WITH OTHERS

TRIP HIGHLIGHTS :

-
-
-

MEMORABLE MEAL : ☐ IT WAS AMAZING ☐ IT WAS AWFUL

A MOMENT I'LL NEVER FORGET :

NEW EXPERIENCES OR LESSONS LEARNED :

MUSIC, SONGS, OR SOUNDS THAT REMIND ME OF THIS TRIP :

IF I COULD DO THIS TRIP OVER, HERE'S WHAT I'D DO DIFFERENTLY :

WHAT I'M GRATEFUL FOR ABOUT THIS JOURNEY :

HOW I'D RATE THIS TRIP : ☆☆☆☆☆	PLAN TO RETURN? ☐ YES ☐ NO

DESTINATION :

DATE(S) :

STAYED HERE :

☐ TRAVELED SOLO

☐ TRAVELED WITH OTHERS

TRIP HIGHLIGHTS :

-
-
-

MEMORABLE MEAL : ☐ IT WAS AMAZING ☐ IT WAS AWFUL

A MOMENT I'LL NEVER FORGET :

NEW EXPERIENCES OR LESSONS LEARNED :

MUSIC, SONGS, OR SOUNDS THAT REMIND ME OF THIS TRIP :

IF I COULD DO THIS TRIP OVER, HERE'S WHAT I'D DO DIFFERENTLY :

WHAT I'M GRATEFUL FOR ABOUT THIS JOURNEY :

HOW I'D RATE THIS TRIP : ☆☆☆☆☆	PLAN TO RETURN? ☐ YES ☐ NO

DESTINATION :

DATE(S) :

STAYED HERE :

☐ TRAVELED SOLO

☐ TRAVELED WITH OTHERS

TRIP HIGHLIGHTS :

-
-
-

MEMORABLE MEAL : ☐ IT WAS AMAZING ☐ IT WAS AWFUL

A MOMENT I'LL NEVER FORGET :

NEW EXPERIENCES OR LESSONS LEARNED :

MUSIC, SONGS, OR SOUNDS THAT REMIND ME OF THIS TRIP :

IF I COULD DO THIS TRIP OVER, HERE'S WHAT I'D DO DIFFERENTLY :

WHAT I'M GRATEFUL FOR ABOUT THIS JOURNEY :

HOW I'D RATE THIS TRIP : ☆ ☆ ☆ ☆ ☆	PLAN TO RETURN? ☐ YES ☐ NO

DESTINATION :	
DATE(S) :	
STAYED HERE :	☐ TRAVELED SOLO ☐ TRAVELED WITH OTHERS
TRIP HIGHLIGHTS : • • •	

MEMORABLE MEAL : ☐ IT WAS AMAZING ☐ IT WAS AWFUL

A MOMENT I'LL NEVER FORGET :

NEW EXPERIENCES OR LESSONS LEARNED :

MUSIC, SONGS, OR SOUNDS THAT REMIND ME OF THIS TRIP :

IF I COULD DO THIS TRIP OVER, HERE'S WHAT I'D DO DIFFERENTLY :

WHAT I'M GRATEFUL FOR ABOUT THIS JOURNEY :

HOW I'D RATE THIS TRIP : ☆☆☆☆☆	PLAN TO RETURN? ☐ YES ☐ NO

DESTINATION :

DATE(S) :

STAYED HERE :

☐ TRAVELED SOLO

☐ TRAVELED WITH OTHERS

TRIP HIGHLIGHTS :

-
-
-

MEMORABLE MEAL : ☐ IT WAS AMAZING ☐ IT WAS AWFUL

A MOMENT I'LL NEVER FORGET :

NEW EXPERIENCES OR LESSONS LEARNED :

MUSIC, SONGS, OR SOUNDS THAT REMIND ME OF THIS TRIP :

IF I COULD DO THIS TRIP OVER, HERE'S WHAT I'D DO DIFFERENTLY :

WHAT I'M GRATEFUL FOR ABOUT THIS JOURNEY :

HOW I'D RATE THIS TRIP : ☆☆☆☆☆	PLAN TO RETURN? ☐ YES ☐ NO

DESTINATION :

DATE(S) :

STAYED HERE :

☐ TRAVELED SOLO

☐ TRAVELED WITH OTHERS

TRIP HIGHLIGHTS :

•

•

•

MEMORABLE MEAL : ☐ IT WAS AMAZING ☐ IT WAS AWFUL

A MOMENT I'LL NEVER FORGET :

NEW EXPERIENCES OR LESSONS LEARNED :

MUSIC, SONGS, OR SOUNDS THAT REMIND ME OF THIS TRIP :

IF I COULD DO THIS TRIP OVER, HERE'S WHAT I'D DO DIFFERENTLY :

WHAT I'M GRATEFUL FOR ABOUT THIS JOURNEY :

HOW I'D RATE THIS TRIP : ☆ ☆ ☆ ☆ ☆	PLAN TO RETURN? ☐ YES ☐ NO

DESTINATION :

DATE(S) :

STAYED HERE :

☐ TRAVELED SOLO

☐ TRAVELED WITH OTHERS

TRIP HIGHLIGHTS :

-
-
-

MEMORABLE MEAL : ☐ IT WAS AMAZING ☐ IT WAS AWFUL

A MOMENT I'LL NEVER FORGET :

NEW EXPERIENCES OR LESSONS LEARNED :

MUSIC, SONGS, OR SOUNDS THAT REMIND ME OF THIS TRIP :

IF I COULD DO THIS TRIP OVER, HERE'S WHAT I'D DO DIFFERENTLY :

WHAT I'M GRATEFUL FOR ABOUT THIS JOURNEY :

HOW I'D RATE THIS TRIP : ☆☆☆☆☆	PLAN TO RETURN? ☐ YES ☐ NO

DESTINATION :

DATE(S) :

STAYED HERE :

☐ TRAVELED SOLO

☐ TRAVELED WITH OTHERS

TRIP HIGHLIGHTS :

-
-
-

MEMORABLE MEAL : ☐ IT WAS AMAZING ☐ IT WAS AWFUL

A MOMENT I'LL NEVER FORGET :

NEW EXPERIENCES OR LESSONS LEARNED :

MUSIC, SONGS, OR SOUNDS THAT REMIND ME OF THIS TRIP :

IF I COULD DO THIS TRIP OVER, HERE'S WHAT I'D DO DIFFERENTLY :

WHAT I'M GRATEFUL FOR ABOUT THIS JOURNEY :

HOW I'D RATE THIS TRIP : ☆ ☆ ☆ ☆ ☆	PLAN TO RETURN? ☐ YES ☐ NO

PHOTOS, THOUGHTS & MEMENTOS

PHOTOS, THOUGHTS & MEMENTOS

PHOTOS, THOUGHTS & MEMENTOS

PHOTOS, THOUGHTS & MEMENTOS

PHOTOS, THOUGHTS & MEMENTOS

PHOTOS, THOUGHTS & MEMENTOS

PHOTOS, THOUGHTS & MEMENTOS

PHOTOS, THOUGHTS & MEMENTOS

PHOTOS, THOUGHTS & MEMENTOS

PHOTOS, THOUGHTS & MEMENTOS

KORIE HEROLD

EVERYONE HAS A STORY TO TELL

We firmly believe everyone has a story to tell, which is why we create the heirloom books that we do. We invite you to visit our website to dive into any of the books in our current lineup and get a deeper look at the contents, purpose of the book, who it's for, and what makes each one special.

WWW.KORIEHEROLD.COM